HBJ SOCIAL STUDIES

NEIGHBORHOODS

Titles in this series:

SENIOR PROGRAM ADVISERS

JOHN BARBINI
Director of Program Services
School District 54
Schaumberg, Illinois

SISTER MARIJON BINDER
Global Concerns Center
Chicago, Illinois

PAUL S. HANSON
Social Studies Supervisor
Dade County Public Schools
Miami, Florida

CHERYL BILES MOORE
Director, Staff Development,
Research and Evaluation
Orange County Department of Education
Costa Mesa, California

DR. WILLIAM D. TRAVIS
Curriculum Coordinator
Pittsfield Public Schools
Pittsfield, Massachusetts

DONALD P. VETTER
Supervisor of Social Studies
Carroll County Public Schools
Westminster, Maryland

THOMAS GREGORY WARD
Social Studies Specialist
Fairfax County Schools, Area II
Fairfax, Virginia

ALICE WELLS
Curriculum Consultant
Cartwright School District No. 83
Phoenix, Arizona

SENIOR CONTENT SPECIALISTS

DR. BILIANA CICIN-SAIN
Associate Professor of Political Science
University of California
Santa Barbara, California

DR. IRVING CUTLER
Chairman, Geography Department
Chicago State University
Chicago, Illinois

DR. STEPHANIE ABRAHAM HIRSH
Consultant, Staff Development and
Free Enterprise Education
Richardson Independent School District
Richardson, Texas

DR. DONALD O. SCHNEIDER
Associate Professor of Social
Science Education
University of Georgia
Athens, Georgia

DR. PETER J. STEIN
Professor of Sociology
William Paterson College
New York, New York

SKILLS DEVELOPMENT

DR. H. MICHAEL HARTOONIAN
Madison, Wisconsin

HBJ SOCIAL STUDIES
NEIGHBORHOODS

HARCOURT BRACE JOVANOVICH, PUBLISHERS
Orlando   New York   Chicago   Atlanta   Dallas

CLASSROOM CONSULTANTS

JUDITH BERG
Bamber Valley Elementary School
Rochester, Minnesota

DONNA BINGHAM
Morgantown Elementary School
Morgantown, Kentucky

AUDREY BORDEN
South Ward Elementary School
Lewisburg, Pennsylvania

MARY BRIGMAN
Oakland Elementary School
Charleston, South Carolina

MARY V. MITCHELL, BURGESS
Reagan Elementary School
Temple, Texas

PEGGY A. BURGESS
Edison Elementary School
Eugene, Oregon

JANE BURKS
Jackson Elementary School
Pascagoula, Mississippi

JO ANN CHURCH
College Park School
Wilmington, North Carolina

ESTELLA FRANTZ
Hinks Elementary School
Alpena, Michigan

PEGGY L. HALCOMB
San Mateo City Schools
San Mateo, California

HELEN HOWLAND
Irving Elementary School
Duncan, Oklahoma

SANDRA LEVENSON, Ed. S.
Stephen Foster Elementary School
Fort Lauderdale, Florida

DIANE LOUGHLIN
Antioch C. C. School District 34
Antioch, Illinois

DOROTHY MACDONALD
Brown School
Schenectady, New York

JEAN E. O'CONNOR
Washburn Elementary School
Duluth, Minnesota

SHARON A. PITTS
De Vaney Elementary School
Terre Haute, Indiana

MARYLIN PLANSKY
Lincoln Elementary School
Marshfield, Wisconsin

JILL A. SWENSON
Mt. Bethel Elementary School
Marietta, Georgia

KATHY G. WALKER
Highland Springs Elementary School
Highland Springs, Virginia

PEGGY WEGNER
Erie School
Elyria, Ohio

READABILITY

DR. JEANNE BARRY
Jeanne Barry and Associates, Inc.
Oakland, California

PHOTOGRAPH ACKNOWLEDGMENTS

KEY: T, Top; B, Bottom; L, Left; C, Center; R, Right.
RESEARCH CREDITS: Photo Researchers, Inc., © Jan Lukas: 10. Stock, Boston, © Peter Menzel: 15T. © Barrie Rokeach, 1983: 20. Woodfin Camp and Associates, © Lester Sloan, 1980: 28. Folio, Inc., © John Bowden, 1983: 29R. West Light, © Craig Aurness: 31T. © Alex S. MacLean, 1982: 32B. West Stock, Inc., © Mike Nakamura, 1982: 33B. Frozen Images, © Ron Winch, 1981: 37. © Ron Sanford: 78TL. Cling Peach Advisory Board, © John M. Lund, 1981: 78TR, 78B. © Ron Sanford: 79TL. Woodfin Camp and Associates, © Robert Frerck, 1981: 90TR. Black Star, © Kim Steele, 1982: 91T. The Stockhouse, Inc., © Ken Krueger, 1984: 107TL. West Light, © Bill Ross: 110L. Click, Chicago, © Donald Smetzer: 100R. Magnum Photos, Inc., © Dennis Stock: 111T. Click, Chicago, © Willard Clay: 112TL. West Stock, Inc., © James Blank: 112BR. Taurus Photos, © Eric Kroll, 1981: 113BR. Black Star, © Andrew Sacks, 1982: 124. Click, Chicago, © Jim Pickerell, 1982: 125BR. Image Bank West, © Alvin Upitis, 1980: 139TR. Magnum Photos, Inc., © Dennis Stock: 139CR. West Light, © Chuck O'Rear: 140TL. Picture Group Inc., © Jack Spratt: 140TR. FPG, © Earl Young: 146C. Woodfin Camp and Associates, © Howard Sochurek: 147T. © Karen Rantzman: 147C. © Bruce Coleman Inc., Union Press: 148T. Magnum Photos, Inc., © Erich Lessing: 148C. Archive Pictures Inc., © Mark Godfrey: 148B. Photo Researchers, Inc., © David R. Frazier, 1980: 150R. Click, Chicago, © Robert Frerck: 153T, 153C, 155T. (Continued on page 168.)

Printed in the United States of America

Table of Contents

Unit One

Living in Neighborhoods

East Park

We Belong to Groups

In your life you will belong to many different **groups.** Some groups will have many people in them. Other groups will have just a few people.

You belong to many groups now. One group is made up of you and your friends.

Your family is a group, too. You will be
part of this group all your life.

You belong to some groups for only a short time. Sometimes you are part of a group for only a few weeks. Sometimes you are part of a group for years.

You have fun with the people in your group. You learn new things together.

What are these groups of children doing?

Some people get together to do a job.
Work is easier when everyone helps. The
group stays together until the job is done.

Have you ever worked in a group? What
other groups have you belonged to?

Around the Neighborhood

Neighbors are the people who live near
you. Some of your neighbors live next door.
Other neighbors may live on the next street.

Neighborhoods are places where people live and work. In neighborhoods there are places for groups to meet.

3 Busy Neighborhoods

Some neighborhoods are busy places.
There are many people working and shopping.

Neighborhoods are also places to have
fun. How are these children having fun?

Sometimes many people in a neighborhood have fun together. The people in this neighborhood are having a party. They are learning more about each other. They are making new friends.

4 Special Places in Neighborhoods

Neighborhoods have special buildings. Neighborhoods need to be safe. They have a police station and a fire station. Neighborhoods have schools. Some neighborhoods have a post office. What special buildings does your neighborhood have?

Many neighborhoods have a **library.**
These children are visiting a neighborhood
library.

The **librarian** can help you find what you
are looking for. The librarian checks your
books out, too. You must have a library
card if you want to take books home.

Libraries have many books. Some books are about real people and things that really happened. Other books are about make-believe people and places.

Some libraries have places where you can listen to music. Some libraries have special story times.

Neighborhoods Change and Grow

Neighborhoods **change** over the years. Here are two pictures of the same neighborhood. One picture was taken long ago. The other picture was taken now.

How did this neighborhood change?

Many things make a neighborhood change. When buildings become old, they must be fixed up or torn down. Some neighborhoods grow larger. New homes, stores, and schools are built.

SKILLS PRACTICE

Reading a Photograph

You know what a **photograph** is. It is a picture you take with a camera. Now see how well you can read a photograph. Which of these things are in the photograph on page 16?

a girl	a boy	a baby
a dog	a man	a train
a horse	a woman	a bike
a car	a park	some hills

Things in a photograph look large when they are close. They look small when they are far away.

Look at the photograph and answer the questions.

1. Why does the girl in the blue jacket look larger than the girl with the ball?

2. Why does the boy with the bike look smaller than the dog?

3. Are the cars close to the people or far away?

4. What is between the girl in the blue jacket and the woman?

5. Is the boy with the bike in front of or behind the dog?

SKILLS PRACTICE

Looking Down from Above

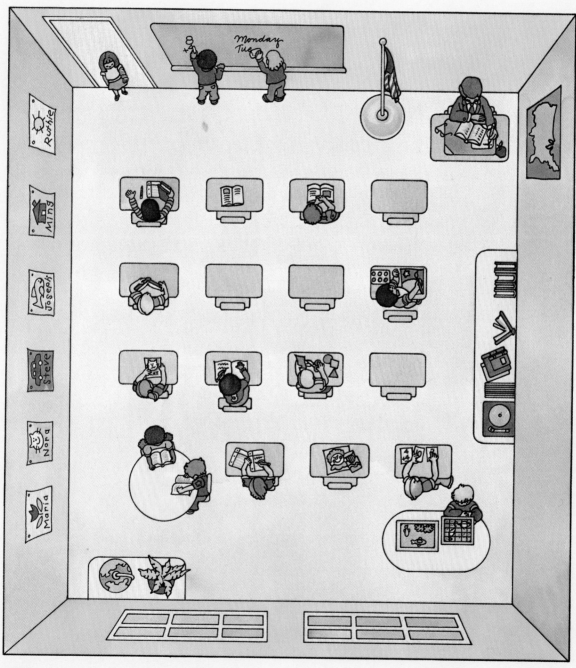

Things look different when you see them from high above. Think of a time when you were high above the ground. Maybe you were flying in an airplane. Maybe you were in a tall building. What did you see?

Some pictures show how things look from high above. Which of these things are in the picture of a classroom on page 18?

a teacher   a student painting
a student reading   a student going out of the room
a student playing ball   a globe
a student drawing   a flag
a student using scissors a student writing

Look at the picture and answer the questions.

1. What is to the right of the globe?

2. Is the door to the right or left of the chalkboard?

3. Are the windows near the flag?

4. What is on the wall next to the teacher?

5. Is the student coming into the room in front of or behind the desks?

SKILLS PRACTICE

Photographs and Maps

This photograph shows how Carmen's neighborhood looks from above. Find the park. What else can you find?

This is a **map** of Carmen's neighborhood. How is the map like the photograph on page 20? How is it different? What things do you see in the picture that are not on the map?

UNIT 1 REVIEW

Words to Remember

Use these words to finish the sentences.

groups	neighbor	library	neighborhood

1. You belong to many _____ .

2. A _____ is someone who lives near you.

3. A _____ is a place where people live and work.

4. A _____ is a place with many books.

Ideas to Review

1. Name two groups you belong to.

2. What is one reason to be in a group?

3. Name two things people do in neighborhoods.

4. Name five special buildings that are found in many neighborhoods.

5. What are two kinds of books in a library?

6. Name two ways in which neighborhoods change.

Skills Activities

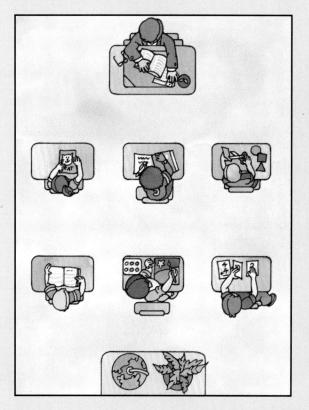 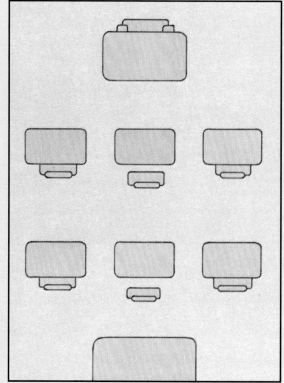

Look at the picture and the map. Then answer the questions.

1. Is the student who is using scissors to the right or the left of the student who is writing?

2. What is next to the globe?

3. Is the teacher in front of or behind the students?

4. What things do you see in the picture that are not on the map?

Unit Two

Neighborhoods Are Different

Neighbors Are Different

Neighborhoods are often made up of different kinds of people. There are people of different ages. There are people from different backgrounds.

Neighbors learn different things from one another.

Neighbors **share** different things with one another.

Neighbors help each other, too.

A storm passed through this neighborhood.
The storm did a lot of harm.

How are these neighbors helping one
another?

Different Places to Live

In the **United States,** people live in many different kinds of places. This neighborhood is near the **ocean.** An ocean is a very large body of salt water.

Some people live near **lakes.** A lake is a body of water, too. It has land all around it. Lakes can be large or small. Most lakes have fresh water in them. This neighborhood is next to a lake.

29

Hills are places where the land is high.
This neighborhood is on a hill. The streets
go up and down.

Mountains are like hills, only much,
much higher. They are the highest land
there is. This town is up near the
mountains. It is cool here. During the
winter, snow covers the mountains.

Very flat land is called a **plain.** This picture shows a plain in the middle of our country. Here the land is flat for many, many miles. It is very good for farming.

Some people live in **valleys.** Valleys are low, flat places between hills or mountains. There are many farms in this valley. How is this valley different from a plain?

Rivers carry water to lakes or to the ocean. Some rivers are small. This river is large and deep enough to carry ships. The ships take things from place to place.

Islands are bodies of land with water all around them. Islands can be big or small. Big islands can have cities on them. This small island has room for just a few houses.

Deserts are dry, hot places. There is little rain. Some deserts are hilly. Some are as flat as plains. How is this desert different from a plain?

This neighborhood is in a **forest.** A forest is a place where many trees grow. In this forest, it rains often.

33

Neighborhoods Everywhere

A **community** is made up of different neighborhoods. Some communities are called **towns.** The pictures on this page show neighborhoods in Napa, California.

A very large community is called a **city.**
Cities have many neighborhoods. These
pictures show a few of the neighborhoods in
Miami, Florida. How are they different
from one another?

Not everyone lives in a city or town.
Some people live in **suburbs.** Suburbs are
communities near cities. There are mostly
houses in a suburb. There are also places to shop.

Some people live in **farming communities.** In farming communities, many people live and work on farms. Often they must drive into town to shop.

Getting from Place to Place

Some people live, work, and shop all in the same neighborhood. They can walk to wherever they need to go.

Many people work or shop or go to school in different neighborhoods. They need **transportation** to get from neighborhood to neighborhood. Transportation is any way of moving people from place to place.

Some people use bicycles for transportation. Many people use cars for transportation. Often people share rides. Everyone who is going to the same place rides in the same car.

Why is it a good idea to share rides?

In big cities and most towns, buses can take you where you want to go. Some buses are for everyone. Other buses are for school children.

Some big cities have subways. Subways are trains that run underground.

Some people live far from the places where they work. Sometimes they ride trains to get where they need to go.

Some people must cross over water to get to work. Where there are no bridges, people ride on ferryboats. Some ferryboats carry cars.

What kinds of transportation do you and your family use?

SKILLS PRACTICE

Symbols and Map Keys

Many maps have **map keys.** The map key lists the **symbols** used in the map. The symbols stand for real things.

Here is a photograph of a real house.

Here is the symbol for a house.

Match these symbols to the real things they stand for.

1. Factory

a.

2. School

b.

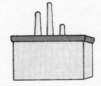

3. Park

c.

4. Library

d.

This is a map of Lee's neighborhood.

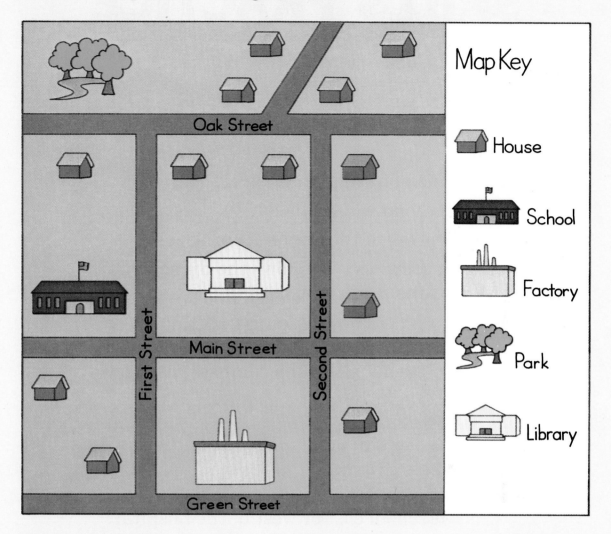

Find the map key on this map and answer the questions.

1. What does each symbol stand for?

2. How many houses are there on the map?

3. What is in the middle of the map?

4. What street is the park on?

5. What street is the factory on?

SKILLS PRACTICE

Directions on a Map

The map on page 45 shows the neighborhood where Allison and Steve live. In the corner of the map is a **compass rose.** A compass rose shows the **directions** on a map. North, south, east, and west are directions. Directions tell which way to go.

Look at the map. Use the compass rose and the map key to answer the questions.

1. Is the hospital north or south of the library?

2. Is the school east or west of the hospital?

3. Allison walked from the park to the library. Did she walk east or west?

4. Steve lives on Third Street. He walked from his house to the park. Did he walk north or south?

5. Allison walked from the park to her house on Green Street. In which direction did she walk?

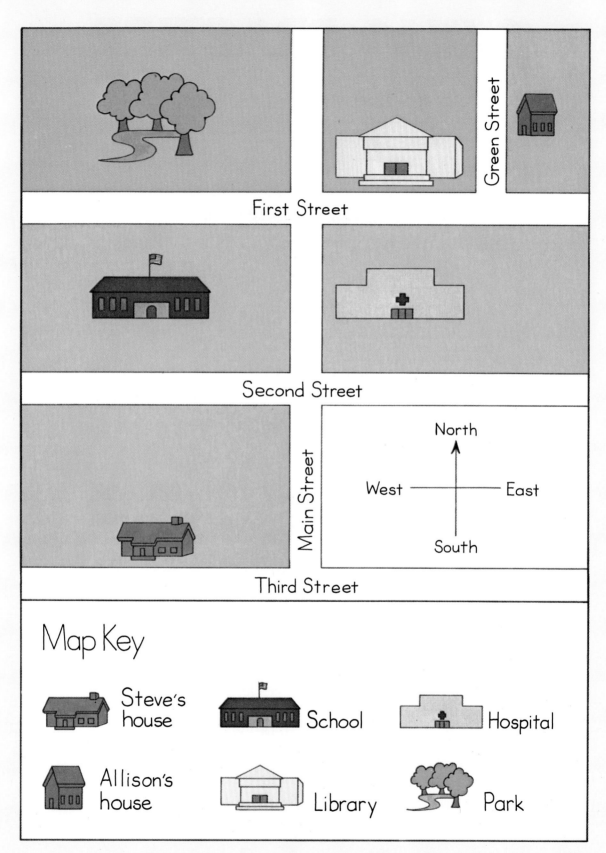

First Street

Green Street

Second Street

Main Street

North
West — East
South

Third Street

Map Key

Steve's house

School

Hospital

Allison's house

Library

Park

SKILLS PRACTICE

Distance and Scale

Maps show more than just where things are. They also show **distance.** Distance is how far one place is from another. One way to measure distance is by counting blocks.

This map shows José's neighborhood. José's address is 54 Bush Street. Find José's house on the map.

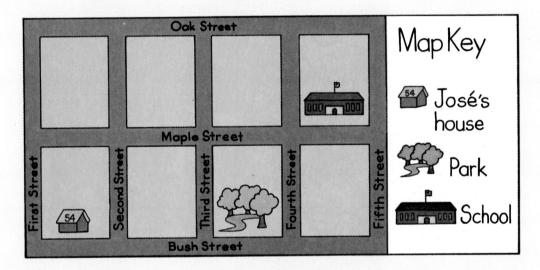

Use the map key to answer the questions.

1. How many blocks is it between José's house and the park?

2. How many blocks is it between José's house and the school?

Not all maps have blocks to count.
Look at this map. Who lives closer to
Lisa—Jason or Amy?

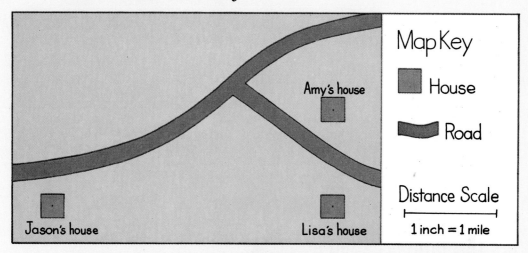

Suppose you want to know exactly how far
each house is from Lisa's house. You can use
the **distance scale** to find out. This distance
scale tells you that 1 inch on this map is the
same as 1 mile in the real neighborhood.

Use a ruler to measure the distance from
Amy's house to Lisa's house. These houses
are 1 inch apart. That means Amy lives
1 mile from Lisa.

Now measure the distance from Jason's
house to Lisa's house.

1. How many inches apart are their houses on
the map?

2. How many miles is Jason's house from
Lisa's house in the neighborhood?

Words to Remember

Use these words to finish the sentences.

desert	island	mountain	plain	river	valley

1. A _____ is the highest land there is.

2. Very flat land is called a _____ .

3. A low place between hills or mountains is called a _____ .

4. A _____ carries water to lakes or to the ocean.

5. An _____ is a body of land with water all around it.

6. A _____ is a hot, dry place.

Ideas to Review

1. How are oceans and lakes different?

2. What is a forest?

3. Name four kinds of communities.

4. Name four ways to get from place to place.

48

Skills Activities

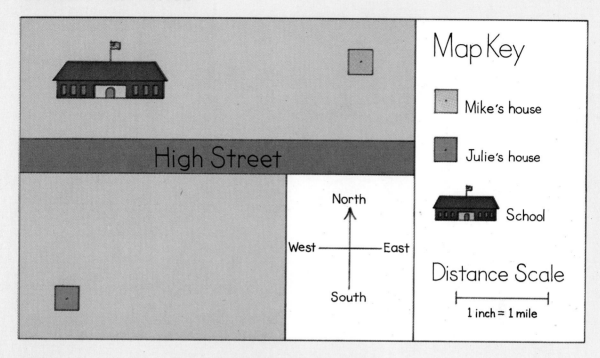

Answer the questions. Use the compass rose, the map key, and the distance scale.

1. Is Mike's house east or west of the school?

2. Is Julie's house north or south of High Street?

3. How many inches apart are Mike's house and Julie's house on the map?

4. How many miles is Mike's house from Julie's house in the neighborhood?

More Activities

Draw a map of a neighborhood. Draw in a map key and a compass rose.

SAVINGS AND LOAN

ONE WAY

SCHOOL BUS

School Xing

50

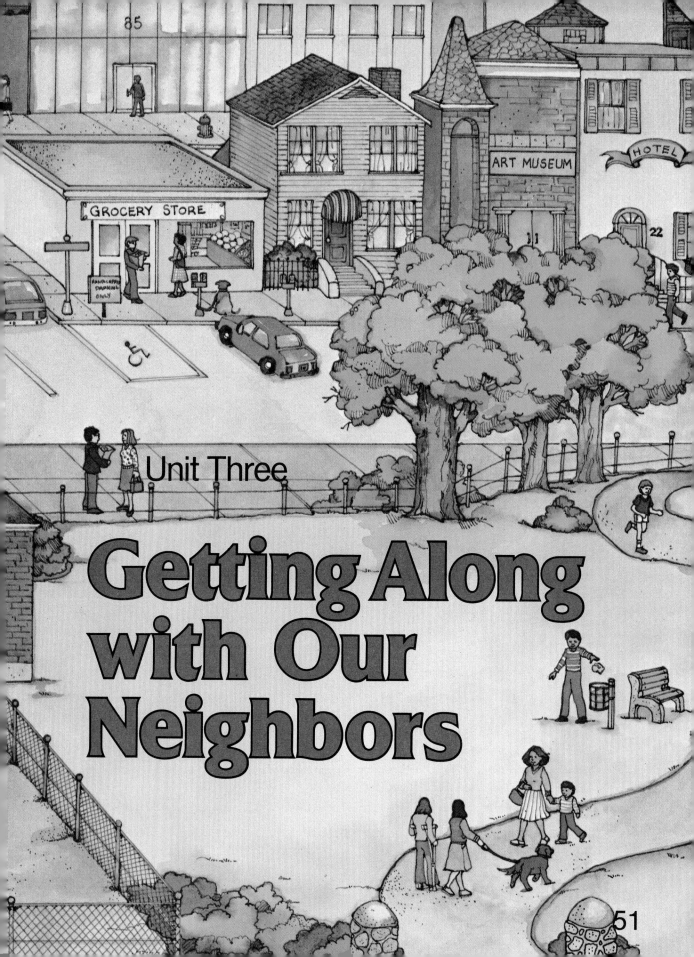

Unit Three

Getting Along with Our Neighbors

51

All Groups Have Rules

Rules tell us what to do and what not to do. There are reasons for rules. Some rules keep us safe and healthy. Some help us get along with one another. All groups have rules.

Every family has rules. Some family rules are for **safety.** Safety rules keep us from hurting ourselves. Other rules teach us how to stay healthy. We have rules for sharing work and sharing fun.

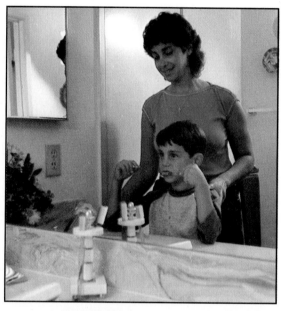

What kinds of rules do these families have?

Schools have many rules, too. Some school rules help keep us safe. We have rules about taking turns. Some rules tell us when to talk and when to listen. School rules make it easier for everyone to learn.

What rules are these children following?

People follow rules in the places where they work. Many of the rules are like the ones you follow at school. Workers get to their jobs on time. They obey safety rules. They work hard when they are at work. They let other people get their work done, too.

What rules are these workers following? What might happen if they did not follow the rules?

Laws of the Community

Laws are rules for everyone. All people in all communities must obey laws.

There are many laws about schools. There are laws that tell what you need to learn. There are laws that say you must be healthy to go to school.

Every day, everyone obeys many
different laws. Laws protect our lives and
the things we own. All communities have
laws about safety. There are many laws
about cars. There are laws about animals.

What might happen if people did not
obey these laws?

3 Neighbors Solve Problems

Sometimes there are problems in a neighborhood. The problems are easier to solve if the neighbors all help.

The people who live on Third Street are worried. Third Street is a wide, busy street. It is hard to cross the street at the corner. The people who live here think that the street is unsafe.

The Third Street neighbors want to do something to make their street safer. They know they have to work together. They hold a meeting at the Ramirez house. They talk about ways to solve the problem. They decide that Third Street needs a traffic light.

Groups need **leaders.** A leader can be in charge of meetings. A leader can help people choose jobs to do. The Third Street neighbors decide they need a leader. They **vote** for the person they think will do the best job. Mrs. Ramirez gets the most votes.

Mrs. Ramirez helps everyone choose a job to do. Some people will talk to the rest of the neighbors. Some people will find out how to get a traffic light. They will talk about what they have learned at the next meeting.

Going to City Hall

The Third Street neighbors know that they cannot put up a traffic light themselves. They must ask the city's leaders to do this. They will have to go to a meeting at **City Hall.** City Hall is the place where a city's laws are made.

The city's leaders are at the meeting. The most important leader is the **mayor.** Other important leaders work with the mayor. These people are members of the **city council.**

Mrs. Ramirez talks to the city council and the mayor. She says that Third Street needs a traffic light. She gives the reasons the neighbors want a traffic light.

The city leaders listen carefully to Mrs. Ramirez. They talk about what she has told them. Then they vote on what to do. They vote to put a traffic light on Third Street.

A month later, city workers come to Third Street. They put up a traffic light. Soon the street will be much safer.

SKILLS PRACTICE

Rules in Our Neighborhoods

This is a neighborhood. Most of the people in it are following a rule. Find the people going to see the movie. They are waiting for their turn to buy tickets.

Look at the picture and answer the questions.

1. The children riding their bikes on the bike path are following another rule. Who is not following this rule?

2. Find the children playing on the slide. Which one is following a rule? Which one is not?

3. Which rules are other people following?

4. Which rules are not being followed?

5. What can happen when these rules are not followed?

SKILLS PRACTICE

Rules and Signs

You see many signs like these in your neighborhood.

1. Which sign tells a driver to stop the car?

2. Which sign tells you to use a different door?

3. Which sign tells you to be quiet?

4. Which sign tells you not to go into that yard?

5. Which sign tells you not to cross the street?

6. Which sign tells you that your dog must
   wait outside?

a.

b.

c.

d.

e.

f.

Some signs do not use words. They use symbols. Have you ever seen this symbol? It tells you where you can make a telephone call.

Sometimes you see a symbol with a line through it. This means that you cannot do something. You cannot take your dog into a place where you see this sign.

Which of these signs have you seen? What do they mean?

SKILLS PRACTICE

Solving Problems

These pictures show problems. In this picture, water is running over the sink. You could solve this problem. You could turn off the water and pull out the plug. You could wipe up the water.

Look at the pictures below.

1. What is the problem shown in each picture?

2. Which problems could you solve by yourself?

3. Which ones would you need help to solve?

a.

b.

c.

d.

Many people help solve problems.

Look at the people in the pictures below.

1. Who are the people helping?

2. What kinds of problems are they helping to solve?

a.

b.

c.

d.

e.

f.

Words to Remember

Use the words to finish the sentences.

| city council | City Hall | law | mayor |

1. A _____ is a rule that everyone must follow.

2. _____ is the place where a city's laws are made.

3. The _____ is the most important leader of a city.

4. Members of the _____ work with the mayor.

Ideas to Review

1. What are two things that rules do?

2. What are two rules a family might have?

3. What are two rules at your school?

4. What are two laws in your community?

5. What is one thing a leader does?

6. What is a good way to pick a leader?

Skills Activities

The people in these pictures are all obeying rules. Find the sign that belongs in each picture.

1.

2.

3.

4.

5.

a. STOP

b. DON'T BE A LITTERBUG

c. Please WAIT YOUR TURN HERE

d.

e. DONT WALK

More Activities

Draw a picture of a street, a classroom, a schoolyard, or a home. Show two people following rules.

Unit Four

Working

Our Needs

All people have **needs.** Needs are things that we cannot live without. We need a place to live. We need food to eat and water to drink. We need clothes to wear.

One of our most important needs is a place to live. People live in houses and apartments. The place we live is our home.

Every home begins with a plan. This man is drawing a plan. The plan shows the different parts of a home. It shows how the parts will fit together.

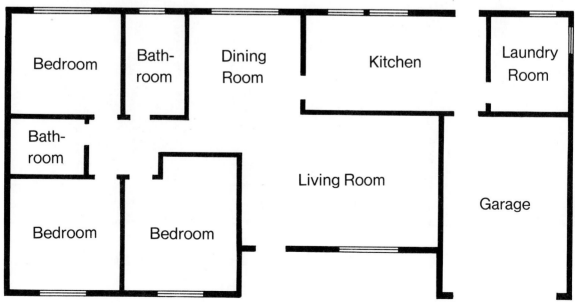

Many workers use the plan. Their job is to put together the different parts of a home. These are some parts of a home.

walls
a floor
windows
doors

wires for lights
pipes for water and heat
paint inside and out
a roof

Every worker does a different job. Each job must be done at the right time.

Meeting Our Need for Food and Water

Where does our food come from? Our food comes from farms. Farmers grow vegetables, fruit, and grain. They raise chickens, cows, and other animals.

Many foods must go from farms to **factories.** Factories are large buildings where things are made. Some factories turn grain into bread and other baked foods. Some factories put fruits and vegetables into cans. Foods can be changed in many different ways.

Where does our water come from? It falls from the clouds as rain and snow. It fills our rivers and lakes. The water is cleaned at a special plant. Then pipes bring it to our homes for us to use.

3 Meeting Our Need for Clothes

How is clothing made? We get wool from sheep. We get cotton from the cotton plant. Wool and cotton are made into threads. Then the threads are made into cloth.

The cloth is sent to other factories.
There workers cut it up. They sew it into
clothes. Next, clothes are sent to stores.
Then what happens?

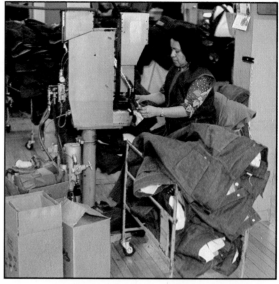

Working for What We Need and Want

Besides needs, people have **wants.** Wants are things that people would like to have. Wants are important to us, too.

What do these people want?

Most things that people need or want must be bought. What do we use to pay for things?

Families earn money by working. Money
that families get is called **income.**

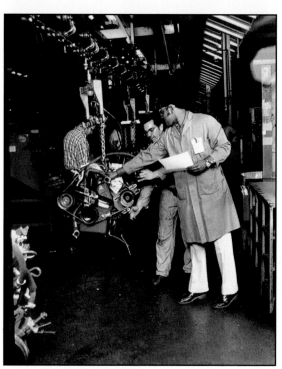

How are these people earning money?

Saving for What We Need and Want

People use some of their money to pay for their needs. They use some of it to pay for their wants. They **save** some money, too.

There are good reasons to save money. People save so they can pay for things they want. They save so they will have money when they need it.

How are these people using their savings?

Many people put money they want to
save in **banks.** Banks keep money safe.
Everyone can save money in a bank.

What would you like to save money for?

Workers Who Give Services

People earn money in many different ways. Some people give **services.** Services are things that people do for others.

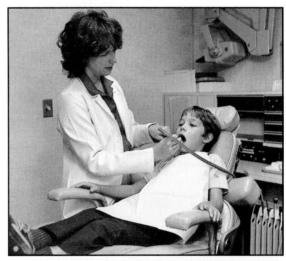

What services are these people giving?

Some people do not earn money from their work. These people are **volunteers.** Volunteers give their services for free. They do this because they want to help other people. They want to be good neighbors and good members of the community.

 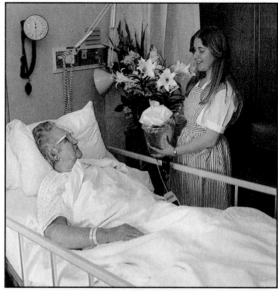

How are these people helping?

7 Community Workers

Many workers help people. Families pay some of these workers for their services. The community pays other workers for other services.

People everywhere pay money to the community. This money is called **taxes.** There are many kinds of taxes. You often pay taxes on things you buy.

Your family pays many taxes. The taxes
go to pay for the services you need in your
neighborhood. Your taxes help pay people
for their work.

What services are these people giving?

Workers Who Make Goods

Goods are things that people make or grow. There are many different kinds of goods. Some workers grow the food we eat. Some workers make the things we use.

Many workers make goods in factories.

Some workers make goods in small shops.

9 In a Marble Factory

Most goods are made in factories. This is a marble factory.

First the glass must be made. Workers fill tanks with all the things they need to make glass. The tanks are heated until they are very hot.

 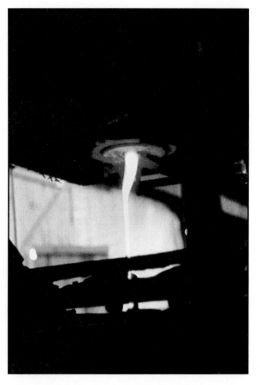

The hot glass is like thick soup. It comes out through a hole in the bottom of the tank. Then the glass is cut into little pieces.

The little pieces of glass go on rollers. The rollers make the glass smooth. The glass pieces turn into round balls. Now they are marbles.

Not all the marbles are the same size. Some are bigger than others. This machine sorts them.

Workers put the marbles in big bins. In
each bin, all the marbles are the same size
and color. The marbles are kept there until
it is time to put them into bags.

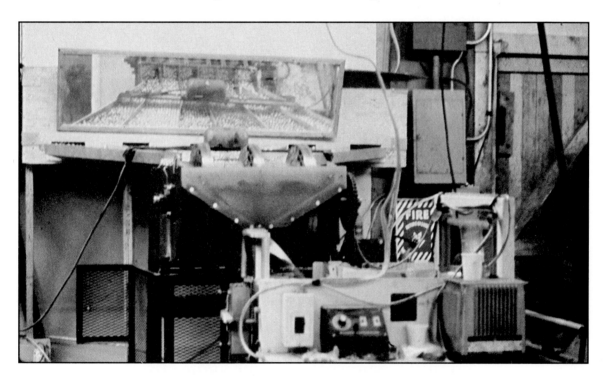

Then the marbles are taken to this
machine. The machine counts the marbles.

The counted marbles are put into bags.
Next, the bags of marbles will be put into
big boxes. The boxes will be sent all over
the United States. The marbles will be sold
in stores.

SKILLS PRACTICE

Putting Pictures in Order

It is important to do things in order. Look at the pictures below. They show a girl getting ready for school. The pictures are not in the right order. Picture 2 shows the girl waking up. This is the first thing she does. The next thing she does is wash her face. Which picture shows this?

Look at what she is doing in each picture. What is the right order for all the pictures?

1.

2.

3.

4.

1.

2.

3.

4.

What is happening in the pictures above?
What is the right order for the pictures?

What is happening in the pictures below?
What is the right order for the pictures?

1.

2.

3.

4.

SKILLS PRACTICE

Putting People or Things in Order

There are many different ways to put people or things in order. Look at the picture above. The people are lined up by height. The tallest person is at the left. Who is the tallest person? The shortest person is at the right. Who is the shortest person? Is Julie shorter or taller than Laura?

The people in this picture are lined up in a different kind of order. The oldest person is at the left. Who is the oldest person? Then comes the next oldest. Who is that?

This class is in ABC order. Sarah <u>A</u>very is in front of Marty <u>C</u>ohen, because <u>A</u> comes before <u>C</u>. One child is not in the right order. Who is that child? Where should that child be?

What are some times when people use ABC order?

Put these names in ABC order. Use the first letter of each name.

<u>L</u>ucy's Shoe Repair Shop
<u>S</u>unnyside Flower Shop
<u>B</u>rown's Department Store
<u>W</u>est Side Bank
<u>H</u>owdy's Market

SKILLS PRACTICE

Reading Bar Graphs

Look at the picture. Count the trees, houses, and cars.

A special kind of picture shows numbers of things, too. This kind of picture is called a **bar graph.** Look at the bar graph below. Find the pictures across the bottom. The pictures tell you what is being counted. Now look at the numbers on the left side. The numbers tell you how many. The colored bar goes up to the right number.

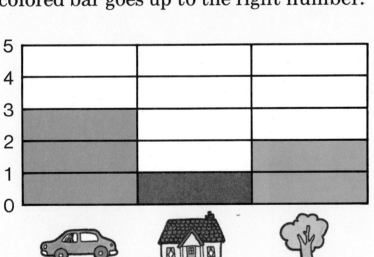

Put your finger on the picture of the car. Move your finger up to the top of the bar. The bar stops at 3. This tells you that there are three cars in the picture. Do the same for the house and the tree.

Look at the bar graph below. Find the bar that shows how many banks there are. This bar stops at the number 2. There are two banks in the neighborhood.

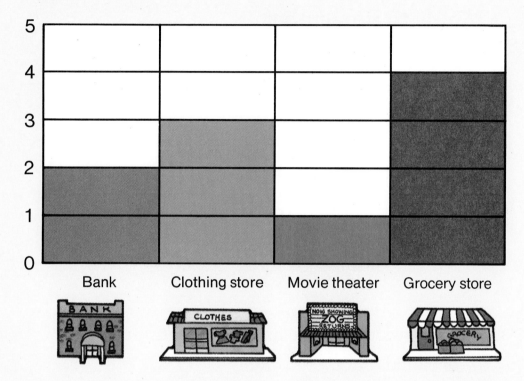

Look at the bar graph again and answer the questions.

1. How many clothing stores are there?

2. How many movie theaters are there?

3. How many grocery stores are there?

4. Are there more clothing stores or grocery stores?

5. Are there more banks or movie theaters?

UNIT 4 REVIEW

Words to Remember

Use these words to finish the sentences.

bank	goods	income	services	taxes

1. Money that families get is called _____.

2. A _____ is a place to save money.

3. Things that people do for others are

    _____.

4. Money that people pay to the community
   is called _____.

5. Things that people make or grow are

    _____.

Ideas to Review

1. What are three needs that all people have?

2. What is a good reason to save money?

3. Name two jobs that give services.

4. What is a volunteer?

5. Name two jobs in which people make goods.

Skills Activities

1. Put these pictures in the right order.

a.

b.

c.

d.

2. Look at the bar graph and answer the questions.

a. How many teachers are there?

b. How many fire fighters are there?

c. Are there more doctors or drivers?

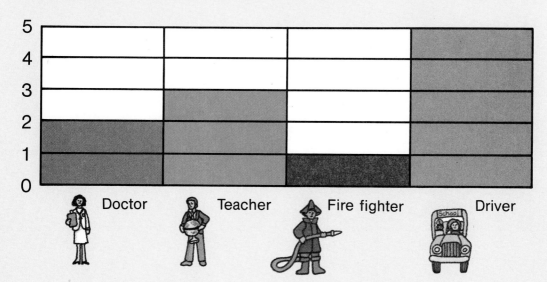

Unit Five

Our Country

The Parts of Our Country

Wherever you live, you live in a neighborhood. Neighborhoods make up your community. Your community can be a town, a city, or a suburb.

Every community is in a **state.** Each
state has special laws of its own. Each state
has its own leaders.

What state is your community in?

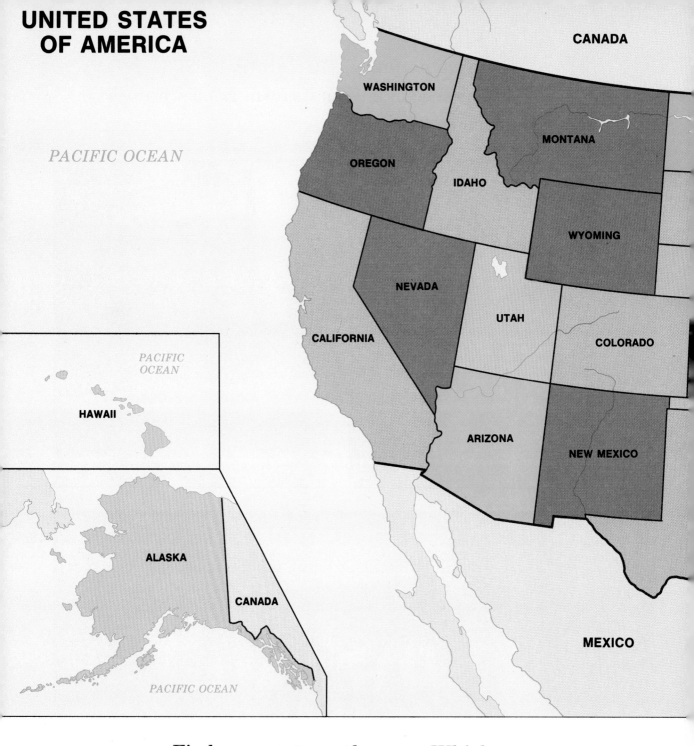

UNITED STATES OF AMERICA

Find your state on the map. Which
states are your closest neighbors? Which
states have you been to?

There are 50 states in the United States.
Two of these states are far from the rest of
the United States. Which states are those?

The Beauty of Our Country

Our country is very large. It is made up of many different kinds of land.

Do you think that the land near the ocean all looks the same? The picture on the left shows the state of Washington. It is next to the Pacific Ocean. The picture on the right shows the state of Florida. Florida is in the South. It is next to the Atlantic Ocean.

How are these two places different?

The land looks different wherever you go. Some places are high, and some are very low.

The United States has many high mountains. The highest one is Mount McKinley, in Alaska.

The lowest place in our country is a valley. It is called Death Valley. Death Valley is in California.

This is the Grand Canyon in Arizona. A **canyon** is a narrow valley with high sides.

No two places are exactly alike. No two deserts are alike. Some deserts have many plants and animals. Some deserts are mostly sand.

No two rivers are alike. Some are big, and some are small. Some run through hills and valleys. Some run through big cities.

Our country has many beautiful places. Some of these are special parks for everyone to visit. What are some beautiful places in your state?

The First Americans

The first people who lived in America were Indians. There were many different groups of Indians. They lived all over the country.

Some Indians lived in towns. Their homes were made of tree bark.

Some Indians moved from place to place.
Their homes were made of animal skins.

Indians got their food in different ways.
Some planted **crops.** Some caught fish.
Some hunted wild animals. Other Indians
got food in all these ways.

Why do you think different Indians lived
in such different ways?

Our Country's Past

Long ago, in a place called Europe, people did not know about America. In 1492 Christopher Columbus crossed the ocean and came to America. Columbus went back to Europe. He told people about the land he had found.

People in Europe began to learn about America. They heard that there was enough land for everyone.

People from England sailed to America. They built a new community in Virginia. It was called Jamestown. They planted grain and vegetables. They had to work hard to make good lives for themselves.

The Pilgrims were another group from England. They built a community in Plymouth, Massachusetts. They lived near a community of Indians. The Indians taught the Pilgrims many things. They taught them how to grow plants. They taught them how to live in the new country.

The Pilgrims' first year was very hard. Many of them became sick. Often they did not have enough to eat.

They were glad to get the help of their neighbors. They were thankful at the end of that year. When they brought in their crops, the Pilgrims and the Indians shared a big dinner. This was the first Thanksgiving.

5 Our Fight for Freedom

People came to America from many different countries. Soon there were communities all along the Atlantic Ocean. There were small farms and fishing towns in the north. There were big farms in the south.

The communities grew larger. They were called **colonies.** There were 13 colonies. All the colonies belonged to England. This meant that the people had to follow laws made by England.

Some of these laws were unfair.
Americans did not like England's laws.
They said they had a right to make their
own laws. They said that they wanted to
be a free country.

The king of England sent soldiers to America. They fought with the Americans who wanted to be free. After years of fighting, the Americans won. The king called his soldiers home. The Americans had won their **freedom** from England.

Today we still **celebrate** winning our freedom. We celebrate with a holiday called Independence Day. This holiday is also called the Fourth of July.

George Washington was one person who wanted our country to be free. The people chose him to lead their fight against England. After they won, he became the first **President** of the new country, the United States of America.

6 Our Country Today

Today, some things are the same as they were 200 years ago. We have a President. The President is the leader of our country. Americans choose their President by voting.

We also vote for other leaders. We vote
for members of **Congress.** We choose them
to make our laws for us.

Washington, D.C., is the capital of our
country. It is where the President lives. It
is where Congress makes laws for the whole
United States.

7 Our Flag

We honor the **flag** because it stands for our country. All over the United States, people honor the flag. How do you honor the flag in your school?

126

The parts of the flag have a special meaning. Our first flag looked like this.

Count all the stripes. Count the stars. At first there was one star and one stripe for each of the 13 states. More states later joined the United States. With each new state, another star was added to the flag.

This is what our flag looks like today. There are 50 stars on our flag, one for each state. There are 13 stripes, one for each of the first 13 states.

SKILLS PRACTICE

Using a Calendar

This boy is putting up the names of the days of the week. He has four more names to put up.

1. In what order should he put up these four names?

2. What is the first day of the week?

3. What is the last day of the week?

4. What day comes after Tuesday?

5. On what days of the week do you go to school?

These children are putting up the names of the months of the year. There are 12 months in a year. The children have already put up the names of 6 months. Look at the 6 months they have left.

1. In what order should they put up these months?

2. What month comes after June?

3. In what months do you go to school?

Paul is making a **calendar.** It shows one month of the year. He is writing in the dates for the month of July.

Not every month has the same number of days. July has 31 days. What numbers will Paul have to use to fill in the calendar for July? How many weeks are in this month?

Most of the dates are written in black. The Fourth of July is written in red. This tells you that the Fourth of July is a holiday. Look at the calendar. On what day of the week is the Fourth of July?

Suppose you plan a picnic for the last Saturday in July. On what date will you have your picnic?

SKILLS PRACTICE

Our Holidays

1. Columbus Day
   October 12

2. Independence Day
   July 4

3. Valentine's Day
   February 14

4. Thanksgiving (fourth Thursday
   in November)

5. Birthday

6. Washington's Birthday
   February 22

7. Martin Luther King, Jr.'s Birthday
   (Third Monday in January)

8. Halloween
   October 31

The pictures on page 130 show holidays. Picture 1 shows Columbus Day.

1. What date is Columbus Day?

2. What other holidays are shown in the pictures?

Some holidays are on the same date every year. Other holidays, such as Thanksgiving, change dates.

First, write down the dates of the holidays below. Then list the holidays in the order they come in the year.

Halloween
Valentine's Day
Independence Day
Columbus Day
Washington's Birthday

SKILLS PRACTICE

Timelines

Sometimes we show the order in which things happen on a **timeline.** Look at this timeline. It shows the 12 months of the year. January is the first month of the year. December is the last month.

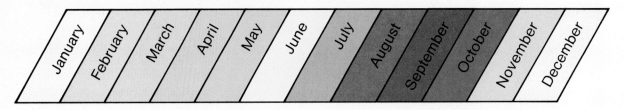

Look at the timeline and answer the questions.

1. Which month comes after April and before June?

2. Which month comes after October and before December?

3. Which month comes later in the year, September or October?

This timeline shows some of the holidays you have learned about. The red marks show where these holidays fall. The timeline helps you see what order the holidays come in during the year.

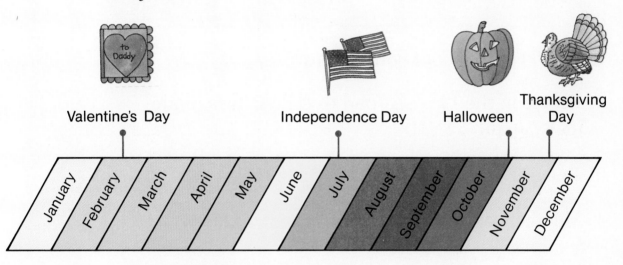

The timeline also helps you see which months have holidays in them.

Look at the timeline and answer the questions.

1. What holiday is in October?

2. What holiday is in November?

3. What holiday is in February?

4. How many holidays are there in July?

UNIT 5 REVIEW

Words to Remember

Use these words to finish the sentences.

| colonies | Congress | President | states |

1. The 50 parts of our country are _____.

2. People in the 13 _____ had to follow laws made by England.

3. The leader of the United States is the _____.

4. Members of _____ make our country's laws.

Ideas to Review

1. Who were the first people to live in our country?

2. Who crossed the ocean in 1492 and came to America?

3. What did the Indians teach the Pilgrims?

4. Who celebrated the first Thanksgiving?

5. Which country did the 13 colonies belong to?

6. What does our flag stand for? What do its stars stand for? What do its stripes stand for?

134

Skills Activities

This is Becky's timeline. It shows what happened to her last year.

Look at the timeline and answer the questions.

1. What did Becky do in June?

2. What did Becky do in September?

More Activities

Becky's timeline does not show holidays. Copy the timeline on a big piece of paper. Then put some holidays on it. Put in Valentine's Day (February 14) and Independence Day (July 4). Then put in your birthday.

Unit Six

Our World

The Earth Is Our Home

People, animals, and plants all share the same home. The **Earth** is our home. It gives us the **resources** we need to live. Resources are things that people use.

The food we eat comes from the Earth.
We eat some of its plants ourselves. We
feed other plants to animals.

Some of our clothes are made from the
plants of the Earth. Others are made from
animals.

The Earth gives us the things we need to
build with. We use these things to make
our homes and the places where we work.

The Earth gives us oil, coal, and water.
From these resources we get light and heat.
We turn these resources into many other
things that make our lives better. We must be
careful not to waste resources from the Earth.

The Earth's Continents

The Earth is a very big place. It is made up of land and water. The largest bodies of water are the oceans. The largest bodies of land are called **continents.** There are seven continents.

THE SEVEN CONTINENTS

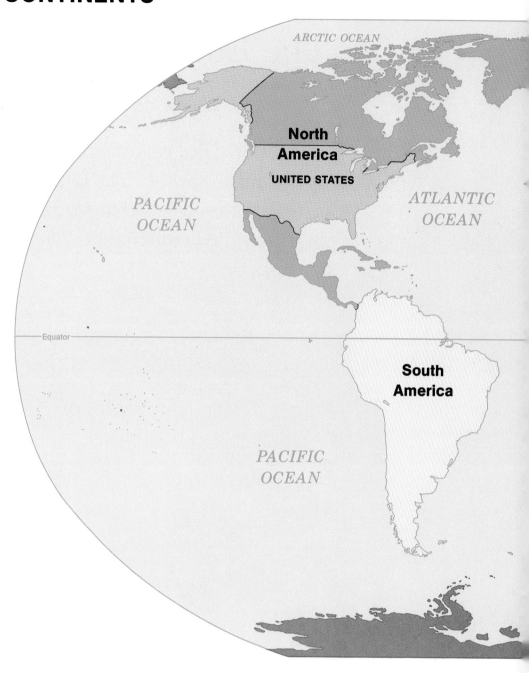

This map shows the seven continents. Find the United States. Which continent is it on?

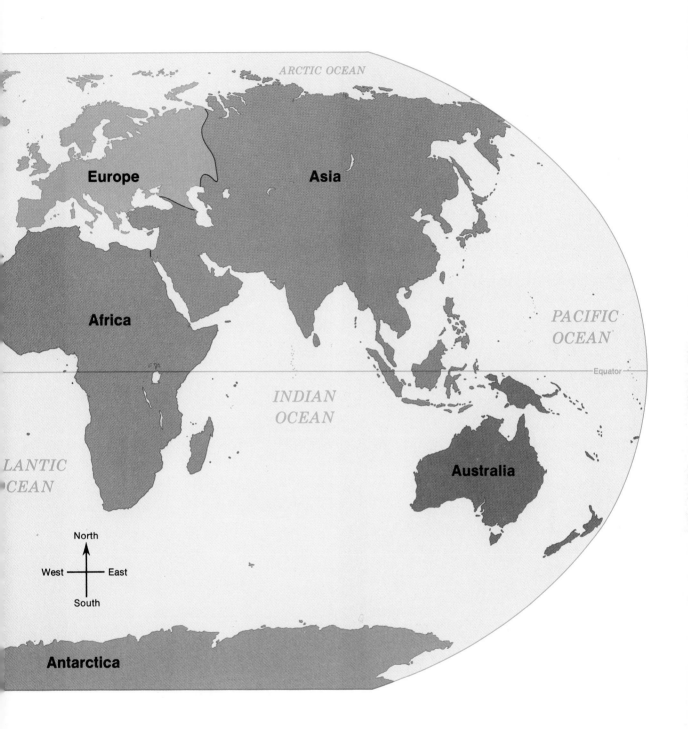

Some continents have close neighbors.
Find Europe. Which two continents are its
closest neighbors?

Places Around the Earth

Imagine flying in a plane over every continent. You would see everything from snowy mountains to hot deserts.

Antarctica is the coldest continent. It has ice and snow everywhere. It has snowy mountains and snowy plains. Once only animals lived in Antarctica. Now a few people live and work there. They live in special buildings. Inside the buildings the people stay warm.

South America is a big continent. It is made up of 12 countries. Some are very warm all year. Some are quite cool in the winter.

This lake is high in the mountains. It is the highest large lake in the world. The weather here is cool all year.

It is always warm in this beautiful city in South America. People can enjoy both the mountains and the beach here.

South America has many great rivers. Some of them run through huge green forests. There are many beautiful places here.

Europe is a small continent. Yet there are many countries on it.

England is one of the countries in Europe. It is an island. The winters are cool there. The summers are warm.

There are many towns and cities in the countries of Europe. Often towns were built on rivers. Some towns stayed small, and some grew into cities.

In a few places there are not many towns. It is very cold in these mountains. Not many people live here.

Asia is the largest continent. The many countries of Asia are very different from one another.

In some parts of the north of Asia there are huge plains. It is too cold there to grow many crops.

In southern Asia it is very warm. Some countries get a lot of warm rain. There are beautiful forests in these countries.

Like Europe, Asia has an island country. This country is Japan. From this beach you can see a famous mountain. The mountaintop is covered with snow all year.

Africa is a big continent, too. There are many countries on it. They are very different from one another.

North Africa is hot and dry. Great deserts cover much of it. People can live only where they can find water.

Other parts of Africa have plenty of water. Long rivers run through green forests. In Africa these forests are called rain forests.

There are also big plains in Africa. Once grass covered all these plains. Wild animals ran free on them. Now, cities are built on many of these plains.

Australia is the only continent that is one country.

Parts of Australia are plains. Farmers grow many crops there. They also raise animals there.

There are many deserts in parts of Australia. The deserts are hot and dry. Few people try to live in the deserts. Neighbors live far apart.

These are only a few of the kinds of places in the world.

Our Neighbors in the North and South

Most countries have neighbors. Look at the map of North America on the next page. Find the United States. It is in the middle of North America.

BIENVENIDOS A MEXICO

Find the countries that are our neighbors. Which country is north of the United States? Which country is south of us? Do we have neighbors on the east or the west?

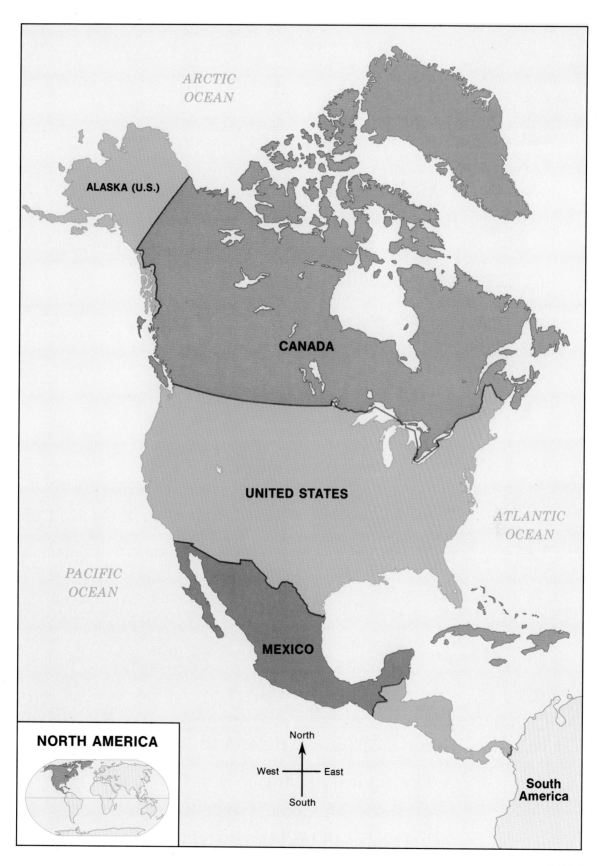

ARCTIC
OCEAN

ALASKA (U.S.)

CANADA

UNITED STATES

ATLANTIC
OCEAN

PACIFIC
OCEAN

MEXICO

NORTH AMERICA

North

West ← → East

South

**South
America**

151

5 Mexico

Mexico is our neighbor to the south. Parts of Mexico are hot and rainy. Some parts are hot and dry. Yet Mexico has snowy mountains, too.

The capital of Mexico is in the mountains. Mexico City is a huge, busy city. It has tall buildings and beautiful parks.

Some parts of Mexico are hard to live in. In the north there are deserts. This desert is hot during the day. It is cold at night.

This land was once a desert, too. It was very dry. The people of Mexico brought water to it. Today it is good farmland. We get many fruits and vegetables from Mexico.

This part of Mexico is always warm. People visit the beaches all year round.

6 Canada

Canada is our neighbor to the north. Many places in Canada are like places in the United States.

In this part of Canada, it is cold and snowy in the winter. The snow goes away in the summer. These people are Eskimos. Their families have lived here for a long time. They have learned how to live in the cold.

In the middle of Canada, there are plains. Crops grow well here. Many farmers raise wheat.

In many places there are forests of tall trees. Rivers run down from the mountains and hills.

Canada has many big cities. Often these cities are near the ocean or next to rivers. Ships carry goods from city to city.

Canada and the United States have been good neighbors for many years.

SKILLS PRACTICE

All About Globes

Look at the pictures at the top of this page. The first picture shows the Earth. It was taken from far away. You can see that the Earth is like a round ball.

The second picture shows a **globe.** The globe is a **model,** or small copy, of the Earth. It is round, too. The blue parts of the globe show water. The other colors show land.

Look at the drawings on page 157. The drawing on the left shows one half of the globe. The drawing on the right shows the other half.

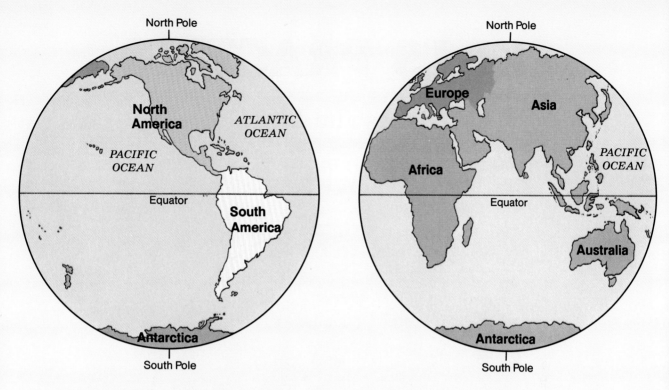

Look at the drawing on the left and answer the questions.

1. Which three continents can you see?

2. Which oceans can you see?

Globes show the **North Pole** and the **South Pole.** Halfway between the two poles is the **equator.** The equator is a make-believe line on globes. Find the North Pole, the South Pole, and the equator on the drawings of the globe above.

Look at the drawing on the right and answer the questions.

1. Which continents can you see?

2. Which oceans can you see?

3. Which continents are north of the equator?

4. Which continents are south of the equator?

SKILLS PRACTICE

Globes and Maps

Look at the drawing of the globe. It shows the western half of the world. Now look at the map on page 159. It shows some of the same parts of the world as the globe.

Find the United States on the drawing of the globe. Then find it on the map.

Find the compass rose on the map. Then answer the questions.

1. If you move your finger from Mexico to Canada, in which direction are you going?

2. If you move your finger from Canada to Mexico, in which direction are you going?

3. If you move your finger from the Atlantic Ocean to the Pacific Ocean, in which direction are you going?

4. Which continent is farthest south on the map?

SKILLS PRACTICE

Day and Night

As you stand on Earth, the sun seems to rise in the east. It seems to go down in the west. This is one way of telling directions.

However, the sun does not really move. The Earth moves. Once each day the Earth turns all the way around. It is always turning. This is what causes day and night.

Light can shine on only part of the Earth at a time. As the Earth turns, half of the Earth is always light and the other half is always dark. It is day on the part of the Earth facing the sun. It is night on the part facing away from the sun.

1. Look at picture 1.
   Is it day or night in North America?

2. Look at picture 2.
   It is day on two continents. Which two continents are those?

3. Look at picture 3.
   All of one continent is facing the sun. Which continent is that?

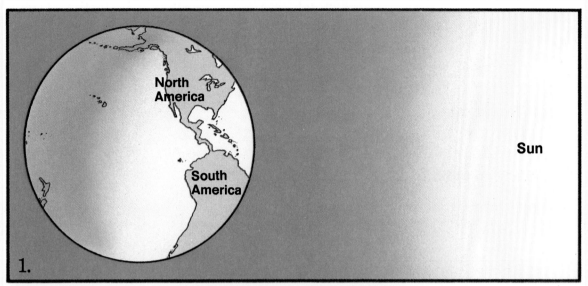

1.

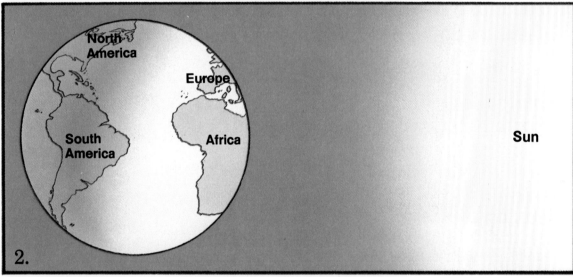

2.

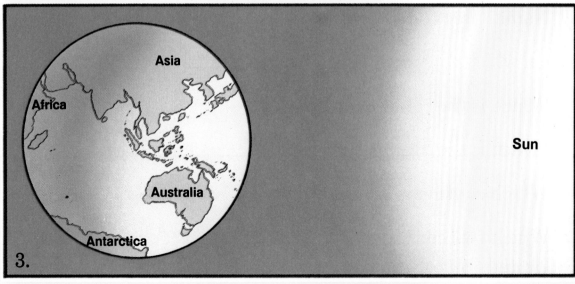

3.

UNIT 6 REVIEW

Words to Remember

Use these words to finish the sentences.

continent	Earth	resources

1. The Earth gives us the _____ we need to live.

2. The _____ is made up of land and water.

3. North America is a _____.

Ideas to Review

1. How many continents are there?

2. Name three continents.

3. On which continent is the United States?

4. Which is the coldest continent?

5. Which is the biggest continent?

6. Which continent is one country?

7. Which two countries are neighbors of the United States?

162

Skills Activities

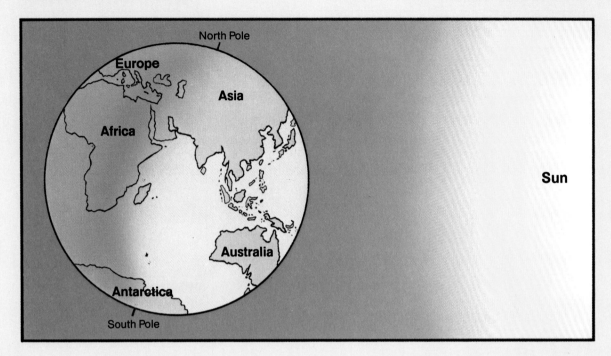

Look at the picture and answer the questions.

1. Does the picture show a map or a globe?

2. Is Europe north or south of Africa?

3. Is Australia east or west of Africa?

4. Is it day or night in Australia?

5. Is it day or night in Africa?

More Activities

Look at a globe in your classroom. Name the countries in Africa that the equator goes through. Name the countries in South America that the equator goes through.

GLOSSARY

bar graph (p. 100)
A picture that shows how much or how many.

calendar (p. 129)
A calendar shows the days and months in a year.

change (p. 14)
To make different or to become different.

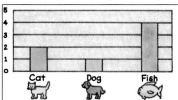

city (p. 35)
A very large community.

community (p. 34)
A group of different neighborhoods.

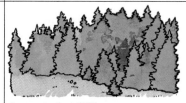

continents (p. 141)
The seven largest bodies of land on Earth.

desert (p. 33)
A dry, hot place where very little rain falls.

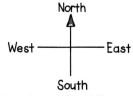

directions (p. 44)
North, south, east, and west are directions.

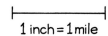

distance scale (p. 47)
A line on a map that helps you tell how far apart places are.

equator (p. 157)
A make-believe line on globes.

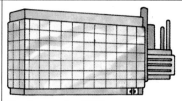

factory (p. 78)
A large building where things are made.

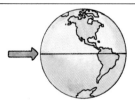

forest (p. 33)
A place where many trees grow.

globe (p. 156)
A model of the Earth.

group (p. 2)
A number of people together.

island (p. 32)
A body of land with water all around it.

lake (p. 29)
A body of water with land all around it.

laws (p. 56)
Rules that everyone must obey.

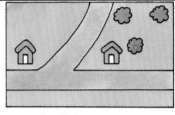

map (p. 21)
A picture of a place.

map key (p. 42)
A list of symbols used on a map.

mountain (p. 30)
A place where the land is very high.

neighborhood (p. 7)
A place where people live and work.

neighbors (p. 6)
People who live near each other.

plain (p. 31)
A place where the land is very flat.

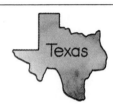

state (p. 107)
One of the 50 parts of the United States.

suburb (p. 36)
A community near a city.

symbol (p. 42)
A drawing that stands for something real.

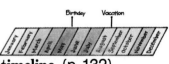

timeline (p. 132)
A line marked to show in what order things happened.

town (p. 34)
A community smaller than a city.

transportation (p. 39)
Any way of moving people or things from place to place.

United States (p. 29)
The country we live in.

Index

PHOTOGRAPH ACKNOWLEDGMENTS

KEY: T, Top; B, Bottom; L, Left; C, Center; R, Right.

HBJ PHOTOS: 52, 80, 81BR, 86TL, 90B.

HBJ PHOTOS by Erik Arnesen: 4T, 67T, 77T, 83BR, 87TL.

HBJ PHOTOS by Rick Der: 66TR, 67CR, 67BL, 127B.

HBJ PHOTOS by Alec Duncan: 3T, 7T, 11T, 11BR, 16, 26, 27TL, 34, 38, 42, 77BR, courtesy of Levi Strauss & Co.: 81T, 81BL, 84L, 86BR, 89BL, 91BR, 95B, 106.

HBJ PHOTO by Susan Lohwasser: 30T.

HBJ PHOTO by Phiz Mezey: 57TR.

HBJ PHOTO by Norman Prince: 66TC.

HBJ PHOTO by Bob Powals: 89TR.

HBJ PHOTOS by Karen Rantzman: 2, 3B, 4BL, 5, 6, 8, 9, 12, 13, 27B, 39, 40T, 41, 42, 53, 54, 55, 56, 57TL, 57R, 66TL, 66BL, 67T, 67BR, 74, 75T, 76T, 77B, 79BR, 82, 83T, 83BL, 84R, 85, 86TR, 87B, 88, 89TL, 89BR, 126, 140BL, 156R.

HBJ PHOTO by Richard Reeves: 66BC.

HBJ PHOTO by William Rosenthal: 66BR.

HBJ PHOTOS by Elliott Varner Smith: 11BL, 77BL, 86BL, 87TL.

HBJ PHOTO by William L. Youngblood: 140BR.

RESEARCH CREDITS: Girl Scouts of the United States of America, Nansi Bauman: 4BR. Sygma, Artie Grace: 7B. Greg Gaar: 14. Tom Tracy: 15B. After-Image, Wayne Rowe: 29L. Jerry Jacka: 30B. Grant Heilman: 31B. Atoz Images, Albert Bendelius: 32T. Jerry Jacka: 33T. Metropolitan Dade County, Florida, Bohdan Hrynewych: 35. FPG, J. McWee: 36. Lawrence Migdale: 40B. FPG, William R. Wilson: 79TR. Department of Water, City of Chicago: 79BL. The National Cotton Council of America: 80TR. USDA: 80B. Grant Heilman Photography, John Colwell: 90TL. Norman Prince: 91BL. Marble King, Ron Montgomery: 92, 93, 94, 95T. Minnesota Department of Transportation: 107TR. Indiana Department of Commerce: 107B. Death Valley National Monument, Joel I. Mur: 111C. Bruce Coleman, Gene Ahrens: 111B. Atoz Images, Celeste Coon: 112TR. Grand Teton National Park: 112BL. FPG, William R. Wilson: 113TL. Tom Tracy: 113TR. FPG, Dennis Hallinan: 113BL. Historical Picture Service: 114. The Metropolitan Museum of Art, Rogers Fund, 1907, *The Rocky Mountains,* Albert Bierstadt: 115T. The Royal Ontario Museum, Toronto, Canada, detail from *The Falls at Colville:* 115B. Peabody Museum of Salem, photo by Mark Sexton, *Appleton's Wharf:* 120L. From the collections of The Louisiana State Museum, *Olivier Plantation:* 120R. Kennedy Galleries, Inc., *The Raising of the Liberty Pole,* J. McRae: 121. Cliche Musees Nationaux, Paris, *Surrender at Yorktown,* Louis-Nicolas von Blarenberghe: 122. Art Collection of the Union League of Philadelphia: 123. Gwendolyn Stewart: 125T. Atoz Images, Sam Griffith: 125BL. Smithsonian Institution: 127T. Stock, Boston: 138. Image Bank West, G. Brimacombe: 139TL. USDA: 139CL. FPG, D. C. Lowe: 139BL. Atoz Images, L. L. T. Rhodes: 139BR. Grant Heilman: 140TBR. NASA: 141. FPG, R. Harrington: 144L. Photri: 144R. After-Image, Steve Vidler: 145T. FPG, Foto Messerschmidt: 145C. Tom Tracy: 145B. FPG, R. Dorman: 146T. Atoz Images, 146B. Photri: 147B. FPG, Douglas Baglin: 149T. Photri: F. Prenzel: 149B. Alec Duncan: 150L. The Stock Market, Richard Steedman: 152L. FPG, Jerry Jacka: 152R. FPG, E. E. Otto: 153B. Frozen Images, Jim Brandenburg: 154. National Film Board of Canada: 155C. Photri: 155B. NASA: 156L.

ART ACKNOWLEDGMENTS

Rosemary Deasy: 68, 69, 71, 96, 100, 101, 103, 128, 129. Walter Gasper: 75B, 100, 101, 103, 132, 133B, 135B. Terry Hoff: 116, 117, 118, 119. Intergraphics: 18, 21, 23, 42, 43, 45, 46, 47, 49, 64, 98, 99, 130, 133T, 135T, 157, 158, 161, 163, 164–165. Susan Lexa: 1, 24–25, 50–51, 72–73, 104–105, 136–137. Lyle Miller: 58–63.

MAP CREDITS

R. R. Donnelley Cartographic Services: 108–109, 142–143, 151, 159.

COVER CREDIT

HBJ PHOTO by Frank Wing